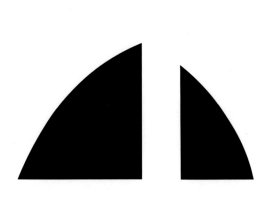

The Human Adventure
a camera chronicle

Photographs and text
by

Norman Cousins

Selection and
arrangement by

Antony di Gesù

For Ellen

who gave me an extra pair of eyes
and an extra heart

Art Directed by Fred C. Huffman

Library of Congress Cataloging-in-Publication Data

Cousins, Norman.
    The human adventure.

    1. Photography, Artistic.   2. Cousins, Norman.
I. Title.
TR654.C678   1986   779′.092′4   86–61940
ISBN 0-933071-07-8

Saybrook Publishers
4223 Cole Avenue, Suite Four
Dallas, Texas 75205

Distributed by W. W. Norton & Company
500 Fifth Avenue, New York, New York 10110

Printed in Hong Kong

Contents

di Gesù

I was sitting in Norman Cousins' office at UCLA to discuss a project I had in mind. As we talked, I became aware of a landscape on the wall behind him. "What a lovely photograph, Norman," I said. "Who did it?" He accepted responsibility. I thought, "Hell, anybody's entitled to one lucky shot," and went on with the conversation. But my eyes strayed to other walls and other photographs. I asked the same question, with the same answer. Seven or eight times.

I'd been appraising photographs and arranging exhibitions for a half-century, and was currently director of art exhibitions at United States International University in San Diego. I like to think I know a good thing when I see one, so I said, "Norman, I'd like to have an exhibition of your work at USIU. Would you let me do it?" He looked at me with a gentle, wicked smile and said, "Yes, I would, Tony, provided you select the pictures and do the work." I agreed and assumed that a quiet weekend at his home would do it. Over a period of eight weekends, I communed with hundreds of 35mm contact sheets and thousands of negatives. It was a delight to discover the endless number of beautiful negatives but sheer agony to have to confine my choice to only sixty for the exhibition.

I could understand why Edward Steichen, one of the three or four greatest names in Twentieth Century photography, admired Norman's work so highly that he urged him to devote himself entirely to the field. The Eastman Kodak Company arranged for a one-man show of his work at its gallery in Grand Central Station in New York City. Several years later, Eastman Kodak put on a second show. In all, some ten or twelve exhibits have been held in various parts of the country.

Pat Howell, President of Saybrook Publishing Company, was at Cousins' home and was attracted, as I was, to his photographs. In fact, Pat was transfixed. "I've just added a book of photographs to my next list," he told Norman. "Of course, I need the author's consent." I'm sure there was a gentle, mischievous smile on Norman's face when he said, "Yes, Pat . . . provided you and Tony . . ."

N.C., former editor of *The Saturday Review* for a quarter century, author of some eighteen books, Adjunct Professor in the School of Medicine, is a restless spirit who has travelled the world many times over. He has represented Presidents on some of these journeys. To quote his physician, the late Dr. William M. Hitzig, "The side of Norman that has commanded the most attention is his commitment to a world without war." It is this commitment that has earned him the United Nations Peace Medal, Honorary Citizenship in Hiroshima, the Eleanor Roosevelt Peace Prize, and the Family of Man Award. But there is another side to N.C. — his ability to capture and work with creative symbolism, which is characteristic of so much of his photography.

The "text" on the left-hand pages, except in a few instances, is unrelated to the photographs on the right. I have selected these passages from the writings of N.C. over the years, whether from books or articles or editorials. These winnowings were chosen for their symbolic connection to the basic theme of the book, as reflected in the title.

Tony di Gesù's connection with this volume both precedes and transcends his general editorial and supervisory functions. He was part of *The Saturday Review* during the years when photography was a major element in our editorial program. Jack Cominsky, our publisher, put his characteristic enthusiasm behind a feature called "Photography in the Fine Arts." The Metropolitan Museum of Art in New York City, in cooperation with *The Saturday Review*, sponsored an annual exhibition of photographs selected for publication in a special issue of the magazine. Ivan Dmitri was the primary force in carrying on the project, but Tony di Gesù's cover portraits for the magazine were perhaps the best ongoing evidence of SR's regard for photography as a fine art.

My own active involvement with photography goes back some thirty years when Horace Sutton, then the associate editor of SR who rescued travel writing from processed publicity handouts and elevated it to the status of serious journalism, taught me how to use a Rolleiflex camera. What especially interested me in its use was its wide variety of options. By adjusting the amount of light entering the lens, by changing the shutter speed, and by adjusting the focus, it was possible to work with film as one might work with paint brushes. The background could be softened or blurred or converted into a texture, highlighting or softening the object in the foreground. The unique advantage of all these special features of the camera was that it enabled you to see things not readily seen by the human eye. Indeed, the main value of the camera was not just that it gave substance to memory by making a visual record but that it also enabled you to see more deeply into the surrounding world. It provided nutrients for the imagination.

As young children, we would change the shape of clouds just in the way we squinted. Our eyes played wonderful games with reality and gave the senses abundant materials for speculation. What fascinated me the most about the camera was the way it could be made to squint along with the human eye. Yet another attribute of the camera was its ability to liberate objects from context and give them a life of their own. I found myself drawn to the barks of trees. In Sydney, Australia, I saw a squiggle bark tree. Dark brown "stains" in the bark contrasted with surrounding tan and pink. Looking through the lens of the camera, and taking in only a small area of the bark, I focused on a section approximately two feet by three feet. The frame completely separated the object from its natural environment. Now I was looking at what appeared to be a cave painting with shadowy figures against a mottled wall (page 89).

Since that experience with a squiggle bark in Australia, I have scrutinized the faces of trees all over the world. In them, I have discovered mountain streams, rolling meadows, and formations that suggested abstract art. Usually, when we look at trees, our eyes identify the object by taking in its general or overall form. But the camera, with its ability to concentrate on a small area, eliminating context, makes it possible to ignite the imagination and witness all sorts of natural artistry.

The reader will observe, in addition to tree barks, other themes that are emphasized in this book — elderly persons, flowers on window sills, solitary individuals juxtaposed against massive objects, the moods of flowers, scenes divided by diagonals, people at worship. These themes are a form of visual autobiography, for they tell not only of the things that readily catch the eye but that are woven into one's personal life.

In my picture-taking I have had an indefatigable ally. My wife has given me an extra set of eyes. For example, the photograph "Three Women in a Kiev Cathedral" (page 9) was a collaborative effort. I had already been inside the cathedral and was leaving for the car when my wife saw three elderly women entering the side door. The ladies wore the traditional shawl head covering. It was too dark inside the cathedral for photographs without bulbs. Then, as the women approached the nave of the cathedral and gazed upwards, awe-stricken at the massive tiled mural, a shaft of light from the stained glass windows overhead fell directly on their faces. I didn't have too much time but I put the camera to work. That photograph will always have a special place in my memory.

In general, I have discovered that the attempt to take pictures of human beings doesn't usually afford the luxury of leisurely, careful focusing. Sometimes it is necessary, quite literally, to shoot from the hip. Whenever possible, I ask permission of the subjects. But approval not infrequently leads to a posed effect. That is why it is desirable

to be extemporaneous and unob-
trusive — or to take photographs
with a long-range lens.

Many persons had a part
in the making of this book. Most
of all, I want to acknowledge my
debt to the late Edward Steichen,
one of the four or five greatest
names in Twentieth Century
American photography. Ed
Steichen encouraged me consis-
tently and helped arrange the
early exhibitions of my work.
Robert Brown, of the Eastman
Kodak Company, was a strong
supporter and arranged for my
first exhibition at the gallery in
Grand Central Station, New
York City. Grace Mayer, of the
Museum of Modern Art, was a
constant source of encourage-
ment and assistance. Bernice
Dobkin Hall, a lifelong friend,
organized and annotated a large
portion of the collection. Emily
Suesskind, my assistant at *The
Saturday Review*, performed a
similar function for the photographs on file at the magazine.
Jean Anderson and Carol Brusha
helped to put the photography
files in order after my move to
California.

Tony di Gesù is more than
the editor of this book. He is a co-
author. He planned this volume,
designed it, plowed his way
through mounds of published
materials in order to select the
passages accompanying the photographs, spent countless hours
working over contact prints and
negatives, supervised the repro-
ductions, attended to layouts,
and worked side by side with Pat
Howell, head of the Saybrook
Publishing Company, from the
original conception to the fin-
ished product. I owe special
thanks to Pat Howell whose
original vision for this book and
whose confidence in it were vital
factors in bringing it into being.

The Human Adventure

The failure to accord the individual human being full dignity is

the calamitous failure. Conversely, the recognition of the need

for that dignity is what makes society workable and life livable.

Humans are not helpless. They have never been helpless. They have only been deflected or deceived or dispirited. So long as people have a vision of life as it ought to be; so long as they comprehend the full power of an unfettered mind — they can look at the world with confidence that they are not living in a sterile or hostile arena.

The individual is

capable both of ennobling

life and disfiguring it. Basic

purpose and human destiny

are not without but within.

The natural environment of contemplation
is not grandeur or cosmic spectacles but
the sense of inner spaciousness awakened
by a connection with our larger selves.

One picture may be worth a thousand words,

but it takes only a few words, if they are the right

words, to ignite the imagination and produce

pictures in the mind far more focused and far

more colorful than anything within the range of

electronic communication.

Convictions are potent when they are shared.

Until then, they are merely a form of daydreaming.

The basic energy of a people comes from their creative capabilities, from their ideas, from their trust in one another, and from their confidence in the integrity of their species.

A free society cannot long remain free if the individual loses faith in his ability to respond to creative beauty or in the stark fact of his ultimate responsibility. This is a great deal of weight for individual human beings to carry; but if it is political or cultural weightlessness we are seeking, we don't have to get into outer space to find it. We can find it right here on earth and it goes by the name of de-sensitization.

Who is the enemy? The enemy is not solely an atomic-muscled totalitarian power with a world ideology.

The enemy is many people. He is someone whose only concern about the world is that it stay in one piece during his own lifetime.

The enemy is someone who not only believes in his own helplessness but actually worships it.

The enemy is someone who has a total willingness to delegate his worries about the world to officialdom.

The enemy is any man in government, high or low, who keeps waiting for a public mandate before developing big ideas of his own.

The enemy is any scientist who makes his calling seem more mysterious than it need be, and who allows this mystery to interfere with public participation in decisions involving science or the products of science.

The enemy is anyone in the pulpit who, by his words and acts encourages his congregation to believe that the main purpose of the church or synagogue is to provide social respectability for its members.

One definition of hell that has presided

over the years is of a place where people have lost

their capacity to recognize or respond to beauty.

Human beings position themselves for

defeat if they see themselves as a species depend-

ent upon circumstances beyond their control.

Anyone who wants to pursue the great mysteries

must be prepared to struggle with imponderables

and take refuge in the imagination.

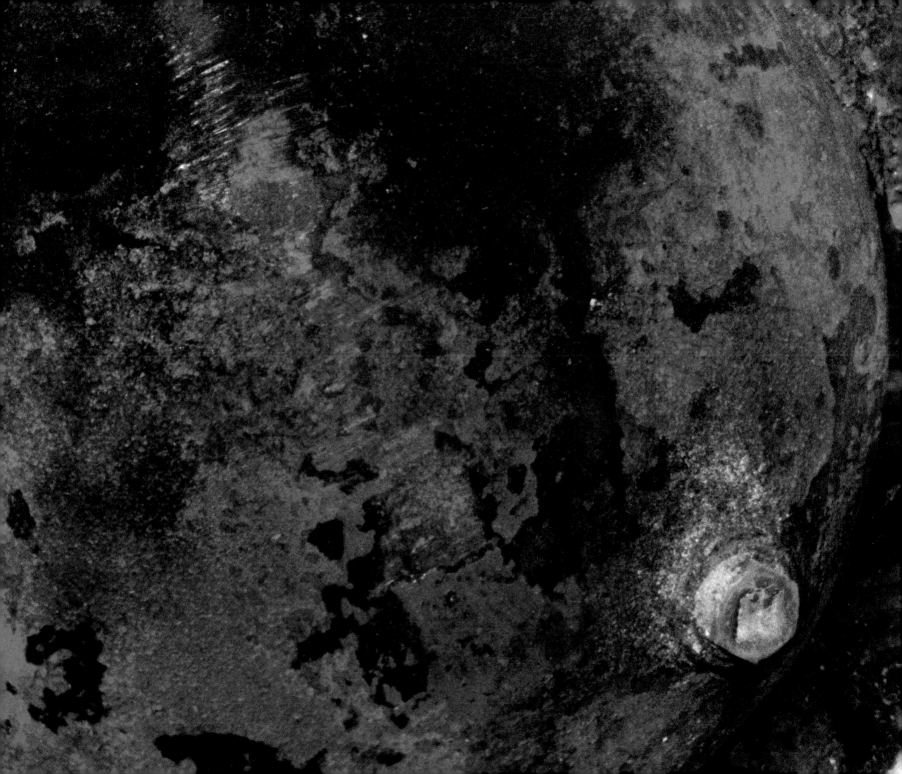

Whether art imitates nature or nature imitates art is unimportant;

they speak to each other in a language understandable to all.

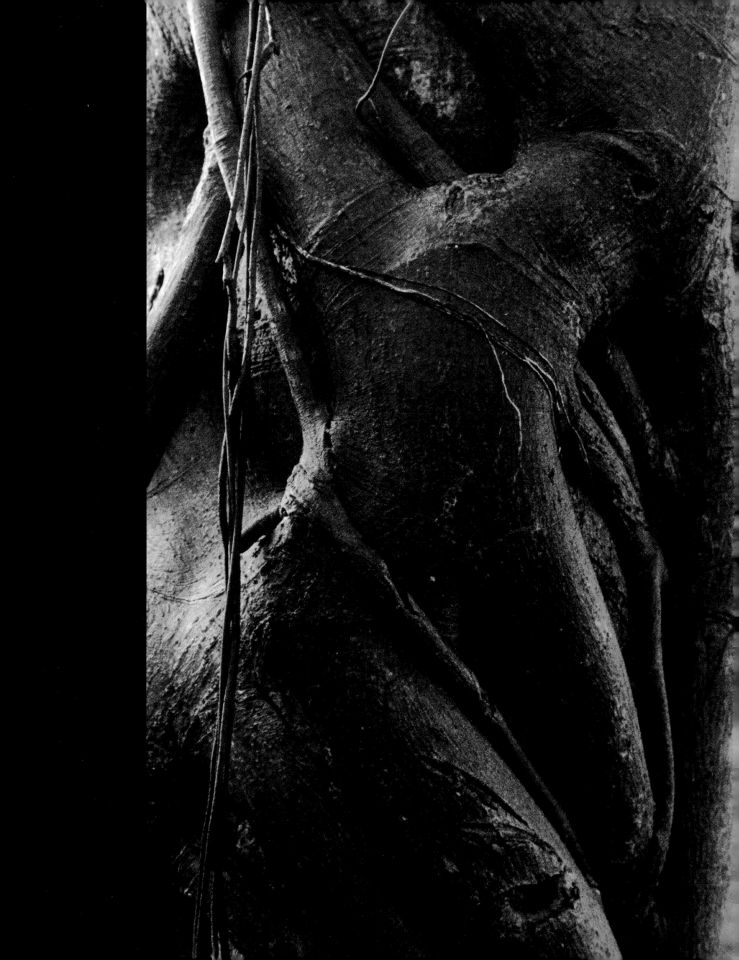

Whatever the intermediate forms of protection afforded to human beings in daily life, the major threats to their well-being and future find them open and exposed.

Life is made not merely bearable but

delightful because of its incongruities.

So long as we have a vision of life as it ought to be; so long as we comprehend the full meaning and power of the unfettered mind, we can look to the world and beyond, to the universe, with the assurance that we can be unafraid of our fellow humans and face choices not with dread but with great expectations.

At the end of the creative process — after all the abstractions and abstracting,

after all the communing with what is known or unknown, after all the sparks

have flown across or fallen between the gaps — there comes a moment when

what is done becomes separated from the artist and has a life of its own.

Art

is a way of producing

creative distortions –

sometimes magnificent,

sometimes terrifying –

that can penetrate the false realities.

Art naturally, inevitably,

invariably, irrevocably,

begins in supreme

abstractions.

Life is precious

because humans can do things

for the first time.

There is primitive, colossal energy in the simply stated but

insistent call by enough people for a situation of reasonable safety

on earth, for an end to anarchy in the dealings among states, and

for easier access by members of the human family to one another.

Certain rights are acquired by a human being
just in the act of being born:

The right to grow
and to meet one's individual potentialities.

The right to appraise and apply one's abilities,
consistent with the rights of others.

The right to one's thoughts.
The right to nourish them
and voice them.

The right to make mistakes
whether of thought or deed,
without fear of unjust punishment.

The right to hope.

The right to justice whether the claim is against a person,
an aggregation,
or government itself.

The right to contemplate human destiny
and the mysteries of human existence,
or to detach oneself altogether
from these pursuits.

The right to hold grievances against one's society
and to make them known to others.

The right to make a better life for our young.

Hope may be fortified by experience but that is not where it begins.

It begins with the certainty that things can be done that have never been done before.

This is the ultimate reality and it defines the uniqueness of the human mind.

It is one of the glories of the human mind that the same

idea or experience is never absorbed in precisely the same

way by any two individuals who have been exposed to it.

Progressive integration is a basic law of life. The development of the complex mechanism of a human being is only one part of a larger being or body that we call the human species. The challenge to the individual is to comprehend this oneness and then live it out.

Reverence

for life

is where religion

and philosophy

can meet

and where society

must try to go.

There are no limits to an individual's ability to respond to appeals made to his natural goodness. It is doubtful whether there is any greater power in human affairs than is exerted through the example of man's love for man.

"The outstretched hand is a basic
form of compassion" — Pope John XXIII.

In the centrifuge of the twentieth century, man is whirling away from the center of his own being. The farther out he spins, the more blurred his view of himself, of what he might be, and of his relationship to the nameless faces in the crowd.

True nothingness is impossible. Infinity would swallow

us up but it cannot. Nothingness surrounds us but it

cannot claim us. The rejection of nothingness is the most

significant fact about life. Not even science can conceive

of pure nothingness, pure nothingness nowhere exists.

Through the art

of creative memory,

the panorama of history

is spread before us.

The grand individual experiences in history can be reborn and fulfilled in the imagination.

We can draw energy from what we do not know.

The deeper the pursuit of the mysteries, the

broader and more nourishing they become.

If our purposes are frail, if the value we attach to the idea of progress is small, if our concern for the rights of the coming generations is uninspired, then we can bow low before difficulty, stay as we are, and accept the consequences of drift. But if we have some feeling for the gift of life and the uniqueness of life, if we have confidence in freedom, growth, and the miracle of change, then difficulty loses its power to intimidate.

Loneliness is multidimensional.

There is the loneliness of mortality.

There is loneliness in time that passes too swiftly.

There is the loneliness of inevitable separation.

There is the loneliness of alienation.

There is the loneliness of aspiration.

There is the loneliness of squandered dreams.

There is the collective loneliness of the species,

    unable to proclaim its oneness in a world

    chained to its tribalisms.

No loneliness

is as great

as that which severs

the society of

human beings

from identification

with the

totality of life.

Human beings tend to live too far within self-imposed limits.

It is possible that these limits will recede when we respect

more fully the natural drive of the human mind and body

toward perfectibility and regeneration. Protecting and cher-

ishing that natural drive may well represent the finest exercise

of human freedom.

The tragedy of life is not in the hurt to a man's name

or even in the fact of death itself. The tragedy of life is

what dies inside a man while he lives — the death of

genuine feeling, the death of inspired response, the

death of awareness that makes it possible to feel the

pain or the glory of other persons in oneself.

So long as the ability to choose

can be matched

o

with options of consequence,

there are strong grounds

for hope.

The wondrous prospect is

that enough individuals

will use their free will

to make the life-giving and

life-sustaining choices.

A painful world we can train ourselves

to endure, but a world that on the whim

of a madman can become a crematorium

or a disease chamber — this is the giant

that steals dignity and reverence for life.

The way the human mind will respond to any given situation

is the kind of intangible that can become the dominant reality of tomorrow.

The differences dividing the nations are serious enough, but they are not nearly so dangerous as what the nations have in common: erroneous ideas about the nature of security; love of the tribe above love of the species; affinity for the collection of power beyond needs.

War is the price paid by nations for the exemptions they grant themselves.

It is unimportant whether

we call Albert Schweitzer

a great religious figure

or a great moral figure or

a great philosopher. It

suffices that his words

and works are known and

that he is loved and has

influence because he

enabled human beings to discover

mercy in themselves.

The greatness of Albert Schweitzer — indeed, the essence of

Albert Schweitzer — was the man as symbol. More

important than what he did for others was what others have

done because of him and the power of his example.

The ability to create order is no less important to human survival than the ability to overcome famine, construct great edifices, write great books, or compose great symphonies.

The human brain is a mirror to infinity.

There is no limit to its range, scope or its

creative growth. New perspectives lead

to new perceptions just as they clear the

way for all sorts of new prospects in

human affairs.

There is no achievement in human experience, no record, no thing of beauty that cannot be rescinded and all its benefits and traces swept into a void.

It is this that distinguishes our generation from all previous generations.

We possess total authority not only over our own time but over all the ages and works of man.

Earlier generations have had the power merely to affect history; ours is the power to expunge it.

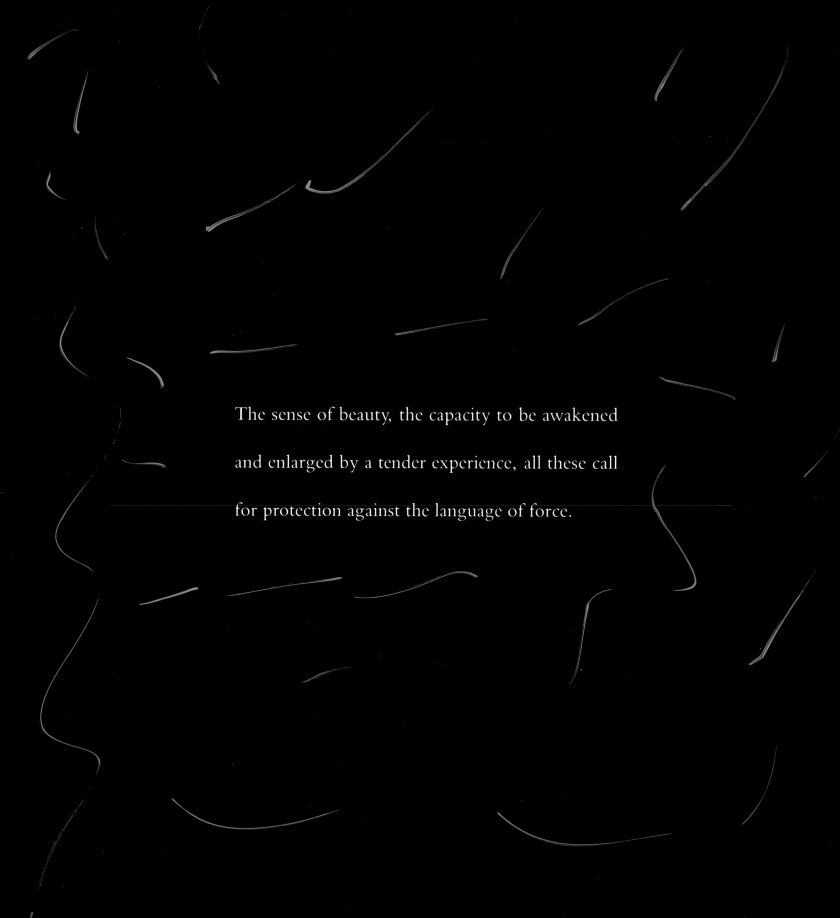

The sense of beauty, the capacity to be awakened

and enlarged by a tender experience, all these call

for protection against the language of force.

Art enables people to have a greater sense

of their uniqueness, fragility and preciousness

than they can experience through intellectual

experiences or intricate systems.

Life is precious not because it is perfectible but because

human beings can comprehend the idea of perfectibility.

No one has ever been able to define or synthesize that precarious, splendid, and perhaps untidy instant when the creative process begins. This is what the uniqueness of the artist is all about. The transcendent right of the artist is the right to create even though he may not always know what he is doing.

Immortality is a living reality. You live in others; others live in you. So long as any human being lives you have life. Your passport to immortality, to be valid, must have the stamp of the human community upon it.

We may sing the same songs the world over and adopt the same fashions;

now let us connect our voices to the concept that our world must be governed.

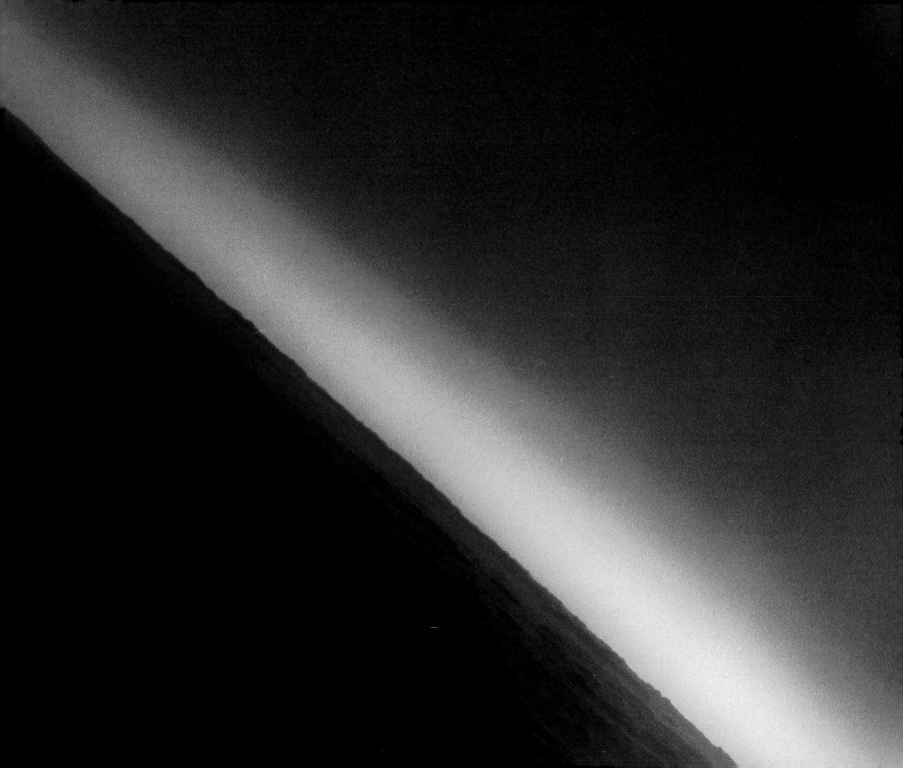

A society can be judged

according to the range of options

it opens to its people.

We justify the gift of life by cherishing the human

habitat and by removing obstructions to its ennoblement.

Life is an adventure in forgiveness.

If I believed that peace could be achieved only at the expense of principle, I would be against peace. If I believed that peace meant surrender to evil, I would be against peace.

I say this though I have seen an atomic bomb explode sixteen miles away, though I have seen dozens of dead cities, their insides hollowed out by dynamite and fire, though I have seen the faces of dead in war.

But the transcendent truth is that a meaningful and creative peace is possible and that it is within our means to fashion a world safe and fit for human beings.

What is most important about life
is that, whatever its place in infinity,
it is infinitely precious.

It is precious not because of any
universal prevalence it may have, but
because it can be comprehended by
the human mind.

We must make our peace with the fact that, though we may be

a highly privileged species, we may not be one of a kind. We

must adjust, finally, to the fact that the universe may not be

constructed for our particular benefit.

Any life, however long, is too short if the mind is bereft of splendor, the passions underworked, the memories sparse, and the imagination unlit by radiant musings.

We are part of the cosmos, but we tend to regard it as scenery rather than a total abode. Even as we ponder outer space, we bear all the marks of specific earth gravity.

Retirement, supposed to be a chance to join the winner's circle, has turned out to be more dangerous than automobiles or LSD. Retirement for many people is literal consignment to no-man's land. It is the chance to do everything that leads to nothing. It is the gleaming brass ring that unhorses the rider.

The unbearable tragedy is not death but dying in an alien arena — separated from dignity, separated from the warmth of familiar things, separated from the ever-present ministrations of a loving relationship and an outstretched hand.

The question is not whether our lifeboat can accommodate more survivors, but

whether, since we are already all in the same lifeboat, we can make it safely to shore.

Infinity converts the possible into the inevitable.

All things are possible once

enough human beings realize

that the whole of the human

future is at stake.

Anything that ignites the human mind, anything that sets the collective intelligence to racing, anything that creates a new horizon for human hopes, anything that helps to enlarge the vocabulary of common heritage and common destiny — anything that does this must never be surrendered.

The size and complexity of problems need not be a cause for despair. If we are defeated it will only be because we became weakened and deflected by feelings of helplessness.

The creative process depends least of all upon accidents. It requires that the

mind be properly worked and tended, that it be given the blessing of silence

and the gift of sequence. Whether the process produces a spark

or a thunderbolt, it is certain to have lasting effects. It can generate the

carrying power to sustain the artist through a thousand nights of torment.

The fact of brotherhood exists. What has yet to exist is the recognition that this is so. Human brotherhood is a biological reality, but it does not yet serve as the basis for our day-to-day actions or our working philosophies or our behavior as nations. It is oneness without recognition that defines our imperfect knowledge of ourselves and our fellow men.

Laughter is a form of internal jogging.

Each individual is one part of a larger being called the human

community. The challenge to the individual is to

comprehend both the oneness and the totality.

Dreams must command the respect of historians. Our dreams, not our predictions, are the great energizers. Dreams put human beings in motion. If the dreams are good enough, the end product will be far more substantial than the practical designs of men with no poetry in their souls.

The poet, and all those who speak to the human condition, can help to remind humans of their sensitivity, and of the need to safeguard and nourish it.

It is absurd to ask the artist if he knows what he is doing. He may not in fact know what he is doing, but this is not essential or relevant to the creative process. What is essential is the integrity of that process.

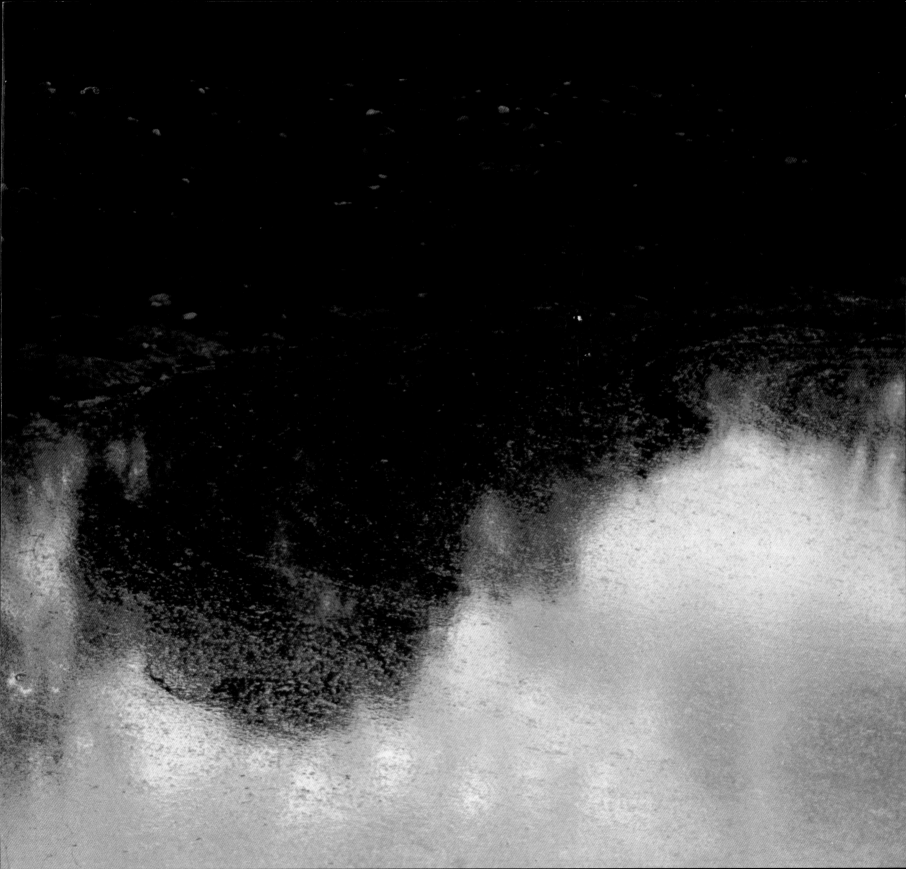

The starting point

for a better world

    is the belief

that it is possible.

Human intelligence now has the assignment of making

civilization compatible with humanity's basic needs.

If this is not done, the verdict on man is that he is a

producer of garbage and poisons, and only secondarily

a creator of fine works, great deeds and beauty.

I am a single cell in a body of four billion cells. The body is humankind.

I glory in the individuality of self, but my individuality does not separate me from my universal self — the oneness of man.

My memory is personal and finite, but my substance is boundless and infinite.

The portion of that substance that is mine was not devised, it was renewed. So long as the human bloodstream lives I have life. Of this does my immortality consist.

I do not believe that humankind is an excrescence or a machine, or that the myriads of solar systems and galaxies in the universe lack order and sanction.

I may not embrace or command this universal order, but I can be at one with it, for I am of it.

I see no separation between the universal order and the moral order.

I believe that the expansion of knowledge makes for an expansion of faith, and the widening of the horizons of mind for a widening of belief. My reason nourishes my faith and my faith my reason.

I am diminished not by the growth of knowledge but by the denial of it.

I am not oppressed by, nor do I shrink before, the apparent boundaries of life or the lack of boundaries in the cosmos.

I cannot affirm God if I fail to affirm man. If I deny the oneness of man, I deny the oneness of God. Therefore I affirm both. Without a belief in human unity I am hungry and incomplete.

Human unity is the fulfillment of diversity. It is the harmony of opposites. It is a many-stranded texture, with color and depth.

The sense of human unity makes possible a reverence for life.

Reverence for life is more than solicitude or sensitivity for life. It is a sense of the whole, a capacity for inspired response, a respect for the intricate universe of individual life. It is the supreme awareness of awareness itself.

I am a single cell. My needs are individual but they are not unique.

I am interlocked with other human beings in the consequences of our thoughts, feelings, actions.

Together, we share the quest for a society of the whole equal to our needs, a society in which we neither have to kill nor be killed, a society congenial to the full exercise of the creative intelligence, a society in which we need not live under our moral capacity, and in which justice has a life of its own.

Singly and together, we can live without dread and without helplessness.

We are single cells in a body of four billion cells. The body is humankind.

List of Photographs

Public Library, New Canaan, Connecticut
February, *1963*

"A Personal Picture Story of People and Places"
Overseas Press Club, New York City
May, *1963*

"The Fall of the Tree"
Eastman Kodak Gallery, New York City
May, *1967*

Colgate University, Hamilton, New York
June–September, *1969*

The Century Association, New York City
January, *1972*

Caravan House Galleries, New York City
April, *1978*

Cathedral Church of St. John the Divine Museum, New York City
June–September, *1983*

U.S. International University at San Diego
January, *1984*

"Interior Images"
Pepperdine University Library, Malibu, California
May, *1984*

"Ways of Seeing"
Public Library, Wilton, Connecticut
December, *1984*

Mingei International Museum, La Jolla, California
January–March, *1985*